YOU CHOOSE BOOKS™

IRISH IMMIGRANTS IN AMERICA

An Interactive History Adventure

by Elizabeth Raum

Consultant:
Kevin Kenny
Professor of History
Boston College

Capstone
press®

Mankato, Minnesota

You Choose Books are published by Capstone Press,
151 Good Counsel Drive, P.O. Box 669, Mankato, Minnesota 56002.
www.capstonepress.com

Library of Congress Cataloging-in-Publication Data
Raum, Elizabeth.
    Irish immigrants in America: an interactive history adventure / by Elizabeth Raum.
    p. cm.—(You choose books)
    Summary: "Describes the experiences of Irish immigrants upon arriving in America during
the time of the Irish potato famine. The reader's choices reveal historical details about where they
settled, the jobs they found, and the difficulties they faced"—Provided by publisher.
    Includes bibliographical references and index.
    ISBN-13: 978-1-4296-0161-0 (hardcover)   ISBN-13: 978-1-4296-1180-0 (softcover)
    ISBN-10: 1-4296-0161-2 (hardcover)   ISBN-10: 1-4296-1180-4 (softcover)
    1. Irish Americans—History—19th century—Juvenile literature. 2. Immigrants—United
States—History—19th century—Juvenile literature. 3. Irish Americans—Social conditions—
19th century—Juvenile literature. I. Title. II. Series.
E184.I6R428 2008
304.8'73041509034—dc22   2007006459

Editorial Credits
Megan Schoeneberger, editor; Juliette Peters, designer; Scott Thoms and Wanda Winch,
    photo researchers

Photo credits
Art Resource, N.Y./Bildarchiv Preussischer Kulturbesitz, 36; Art Resource, N.Y./Erich Lessing,
93; Capstone Press Archives, 55; Collection of the New-York Historical Society, Five Points:
Baxter, Worth, and Park Streets, stereograph, PR-065-0440-0001, neg. no. 70956, 29; Collection
of the New-York Historical Society, Numbers 2, 3 & 5 Hudson St., ca. 1865, photograph by
Marcus Ormsbee, Geographic File, PR 020, flat files, Streets - Hudson, Neg. no. 16930, 16;
Corbis, 9; Corbis/Bettmann, 26, 42, 85, 104; Corbis/Geoffrey Clements, 12; Corbis/Museum of
the City of New York, 40–41; Corbis/Photo Collection Alexander Alland, Sr., 20; Corbis/Sean
Sexton Collection, 23; Corbis/Strohmeyer and Wyman, 98; Courtesy of Historic New England,
photo by S. Towle, Making-Up Room, Lawrence Hosiery Mill, Lowell, Mass, ca. 1865 (Digital
ID# 00982), 62; Getty Images Inc./FPG, cover; Getty Images Inc./Hulton Archive, 82; Getty
Images Inc./Museum of the City of New York/Jacob A. Riis, 31; The Granger Collection, New
York, 47; Library of Congress, 69, 78, 100; Lowell Historical Society/Lowell Museum Collection,
52; Maps.com, 14; New York Public Library/Robert N. Dennis Collection of Stereoscopic Views,
Miriam and Ira D. Wallach Division of Art, Prints and Photographs, Astor, Lenox and Tilden
Foundations, 51, 59, 74; New York Public Library/The Branch Libraries/Picture Collection,
Astor, Lenox and Tilden Foundations, 6; North Wind Picture Archives, 56; Pennsylvania State
Archives, C3-247, #1310 Cramer Collection, MG-218 General Photo Collection, 91; University
of Massachusetts Lowell/Center for Lowell History, 44; Wisconsin Historical Society/Charles
Van Schaick Collection, image #WHi 1919, 66

1 2 3 4 5 6 12 11 10 09 08 07

TABLE OF CONTENTS

ABOUT YOUR ADVENTURE

YOU are a young Irish immigrant in America in 1846. You have no money and no job, just a dream of someday saving enough money to bring the rest of your family to America. Will you succeed?

In this book, you'll explore how the choices people made meant the difference between life and death. The events you'll experience happened to real people.

Chapter One sets the scene. Then you choose which path to read. Follow the directions at the bottom of each page. The choices you make will change your outcome. After you finish one path, go back and read the others for new perspectives and more adventures.

YOU CHOOSE the path you take through history.

Immigrants waited on deck to catch their first glimpse of New York after weeks at sea.

TICKET TO AMERICA

It is May 18, 1846. You spot the coastline before anyone else. Morning sunshine sparkles on the water. The distant land looks golden. After eight weeks at sea, you smile to finally see America on the horizon.

When you left Ireland, the ship smelled as sweet as sugar. Seasickness and a lack of water for washing have made the passengers—and the ship—stink. It's enough to make your eyes water. But even at its worst, it's not as bad as the smell of rotting potatoes in Ireland.

Turn the page.

You'll never forget the stench of rotting potatoes in the air back home. One night last September, a mysterious fog settled over the potato fields. The next morning, the leaves of the plants were black. At first, the potatoes themselves seemed fine. But within days, they turned black too. Almost half the crop was lost.

Potatoes had been a cheap, dependable crop. Like you, most Irish people counted on them as their main food. Without potatoes, there was little to eat. Children grew thin.

Most Irish families were poor and lived in small cottages.

One morning in March, your father handed you a ticket to America. "In Ireland, you have no food, no work, and no money. In America, you might find all three," he said. "Send money so the rest of us can join you in America."

Turn the page.

As you finally reach New York Harbor, boats of all sorts chug into port beside your ship. On shore, buildings jam against one another as if fighting for space.

William Riddle and Mary and Eliza Kelly stand beside you on deck. You were strangers when the journey began, assigned by chance to share a sleeping space. Now you consider Will, Mary, and Eliza true friends.

Will wants you to join him in New York. His sister Kate lives in an area called Five Points with her 3-year-old daughter, Charlotte. "She has a room to rent," Will says. "You'd be welcome to share it with me."

Mary and Eliza are heading to Lowell, Massachusetts, to work in the cotton mills. "You come, too," they beg.

In your pocket, you have a letter from your cousin Brian inviting you to join him in Philadelphia. That would please your mother, but it means another long journey to an unfamiliar place.

As the ship docks, sailors lower a gangplank. You've reached America. What will you do now?

→ To stay in New York, turn to page 13.

→ To go to Massachusetts, turn to page 45.

→ To go to Philadelphia, turn to page 79.

Five Points was an overcrowded and poor slum in New York City.

CHAPTER 2

SURVIVING FIVE POINTS

Will is pleased you've decided to stay in New York. "Follow me," he says. You dodge horse-drawn wagons loaded with cotton, wood, and other goods. Horseshoes clatter on the cobblestone streets.

"Look out for runners," Will says. "They steal your luggage and make you pay to get it back."

You hold your suitcase close as you walk toward Kate's apartment on Mulberry Street. Garbage and animal droppings make a mucky mess of the streets. You wipe your filthy shoes as best you can before climbing the steps to the apartment.

Turn the page.

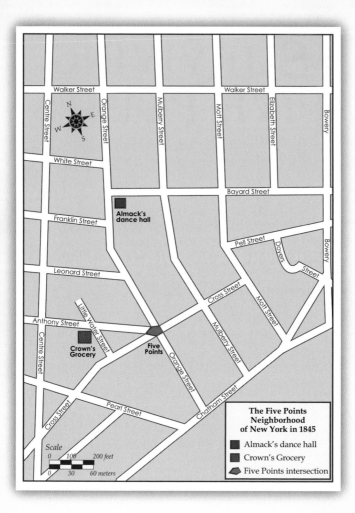

The Five Points
Neighborhood
of New York in 1845

■ Almack's dance hall
■ Crown's Grocery
◆ Five Points intersection

Scale
0   100   200 feet
0   30   60 meters

When she sees Will, Kate tosses her sewing aside and wraps him in a hug. Little Charlotte hides behind her mother. You wink at her, and she giggles.

Kate serves stew. Big chunks of potatoes float to the top.

Kate asks if you have a job lined up. "I saw a Help Wanted sign in the shoemaker's window last week," she suggests.

You made shoes for your family in Ireland. A job as a shoemaker seems almost too good to be true. But you've been thinking it would be nice to learn a new skill. Maybe you should explore Five Points on your own first and see what other jobs there are.

→ To explore Five Points looking for work, turn to page **16**.

→ To apply at the shoemaker's, turn to page **18**.

Five Points is a crowded neighborhood. You pass grocery stores and dance halls. On one short block of Orange Street, you count 16 pubs. You stop in a grocery store and ask about work. "Nothing here." The sign maker turns you down. So does the house painter.

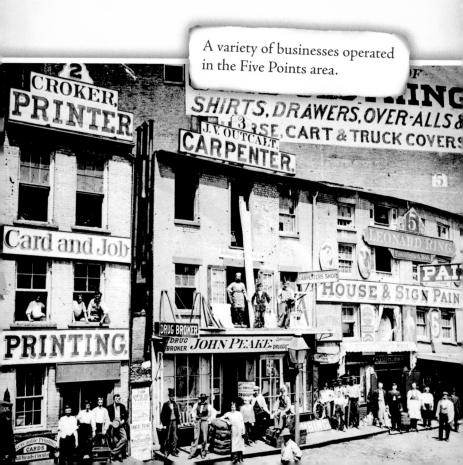

A variety of businesses operated in the Five Points area.

Discouraged, you wander down the narrow streets. Even small spaces are taken up with buildings. The older ones are two-story or three-story wooden houses. Newer buildings are brick.

That evening Will says, "They're putting up a new building on Mott Street. They hired me as a carpenter. They're still hiring men to haul bricks."

If you worked with Will, the two of you could look out for each other. But carting bricks is backbreaking work. Maybe you should see if the shoemaking job is still open. Whatever you choose, you need to decide quickly, or you might miss out on both jobs altogether.

↠ *To go to the shoemaker's shop, turn to page 18.*

↠ *To go with Will to the construction site, turn to page 20.*

Luckily, the sign in the shoemaker's window is still there. With your experience, the owner hires you on the spot. He leads you to an empty bench with tools hanging nearby. "Your workstation," he says. "Pay is a quarter a pair."

You'll be working every day but Sunday. You figure if you work fast, you can make four pairs of shoes a day, giving you $1 a day. Minus the dollar Kate charges for room and board each week, you'll still have $5 left over. Soon you'll be able to send money to Ireland.

The worker at the next table introduces himself. "Name's Harry O'Connor," he says. "The pay may seem like a lot compared to what you earned in Ireland. But it won't buy much in America. We shoemakers talk about going on strike. We'll refuse to work until they have no choice but to raise our pay."

The talk makes you nervous. You don't want to strike. You want to work. "A strike won't help," you say. "With so many people looking for work, they'll just hire new workers. Low pay is better than no pay."

Turn to page 22.

You follow Will to the construction site. You are hired to haul bricks from the brickyard, where they are made, to the new building. By the end of the week, you are exhausted.

You earn 80 cents for each day you work. On payday, it feels good to have money in your pocket again.

Laborers could often find jobs constructing new streets and buildings.

Will invites you to join him and some of the men from work at Brennan's Pub. You'd like to get to know the other workers. A newcomer like you can use all the friends he can make. But you promised to pay your rent right after work. "I need to buy groceries," Kate said that morning.

"She can wait," Will says. But you did make a promise.

→To go to Brennan's, turn to page **23**.

→To return to the apartment, turn to page **28**.

You make shoes for 14 hours a day and listen to the friendly chatter of the other shoemakers. By week's end, your back aches from bending over the worktable. But when you get paid Saturday night, you forget the pain.

Harry and the other shoemakers are heading to Brennan's Pub. They invite you along. You'd like to go, but you told Kate you'd pay her right after work. She needs the money for groceries. Is it fair to make her wait while you go to the pub?

➤ To go with Harry to Brennan's Pub, go to page **23**.

➤ To go back to the apartment, turn to page **28**.

It feels good to relax at Brennan's after work, even just for a few minutes. One of your coworkers tells about the letter he received from his sister in Ireland. She writes that her family has been forced to leave their home. "They dug a hole in the ground and covered it with dirt and grass. That's where they live now," he says.

Evicted families in Ireland sometimes built temporary homes called scalpeens.

Turn the page.

You return to the apartment, give Kate the rent money, and write a letter home to your parents. "In America, we eat like it is Christmas every day. I earn three times Irish wages, but do six times Irish work. Anyone who works hard can do well here, but it is not easy." You enclose a single dollar.

Your life falls into a pattern. You work from sunrise to sunset. The weather turns cold, and your apartment gets little or no heat. Snow drifts into the hallways.

One night, Will invites you to go to Brennan's. "Come on. You need some fun."

"I'd love to, but maybe I should stay in," you say.

Brennan's is likely warmer than your apartment, and it would be nice to see your friends. But you don't want to spend the last of your money. You'd like to be able to send a little extra money to your family.

→ To go to Brennan's with Will, turn to page **26**.

→ To stay home, turn to page **32**.

At Brennan's, Will introduces you to some friends. "I'm a proud member of Fulton Engine Company 21," one man says. "Without volunteer firefighters like us, Five Points would burn to the ground."

You are singing some old Irish tunes when a fire alarm rings. The firemen dash out the door. You follow the clanging bells of the horse-drawn fire engine. Flames leap out of a second-floor window of a wooden tenement on Orange Street.

In the 1800s, firefighters used horses and wagons to rush to burning buildings.

As the men of Company 21 aim their hoses at the flames, Company 22 arrives. "It's our fire," Company 21 yells.

"No, it belongs to Company 22."

While the two companies argue, no one is fighting the fire. A woman standing next to you shivers as she comforts her crying baby. "I've lost everything," she sobs.

All you have to offer is your heavy shirt. You wrap it around the woman and her baby. But it's late, and you're getting cold. You should go home. There must be others who are better able to help than you are.

→ *To go back to your apartment, turn to page 32.*

→ *To stay to help the woman and her child, turn to page 36.*

It wouldn't be fair to make Kate wait. You return to the apartment right away to pay the rent. You also give Kate a little extra money to do your wash.

Kate and Charlotte are going to Crown's Grocery on Anthony Street. "Crown's has everything. Do you want to come?"

People not only buy food at Crown's but also pause for a drink and a visit with friends. When Kate and Charlotte go home, you stay. Soon you are laughing with new friends. "We're off to Almack's dance hall. Join us."

At Almack's, you hear the fiddler playing an Irish jig even before you go inside. Everyone dances to the lively tunes.

Crown's Grocery (building on left) was on the corner of Anthony Street and Little Water Street in Five Points.

Turn the page.

Your new friends are members of a gang called the Black Crows. They play cards and go bowling in the alley behind Orange Street. They always end the night at a pub or dance hall. It seems as if everyone in Five Points belongs to one gang or another.

When you're with the gang, you don't feel homesick. But after two months in New York, you haven't sent a penny to Ireland. If you want to send money to Ireland, you'll have to quit the gang. You must choose between friends or family.

A group of men stands in an alley behind Mulberry Street, a popular hangout for gangs.

❧ To continue hanging out with the gang,
turn to page **34**.

❧ To quit the gang so you can help your family,
turn to page **40**.

Shivering, you climb into bed hoping to escape the cold. But your thin blanket isn't enough to block the winter wind whipping through the apartment. You're going to need a warmer blanket. On the next payday, you find a shop selling blankets at reasonable prices.

"You're my last customer," the shopkeeper says. "I'm closing up and moving to California. Land is cheap. They'll need shops."

He stops for a moment and studies you. "Do you like adventure?" he continues. "I can use a good worker if you want to come along."

What luck! If you were a store clerk, you'd make good money. Someday you might even open your own store.

You think about your family. Whether you go to California or stay in New York, you'll get them to America. But the long trip from New York to California will be too hard on old people and children. You can't expect them to join you there. Should you go to California alone or stay in New York?

❧ *To stay in New York, turn to page* **40**.

❧ *To go to California, turn to page* **43**.

You like having friends here in America who will look out for you. You spend every evening and most Sundays with the Black Crows. Sometimes you meet other gangs, such as the Swamp Angels or the Dead Rabbits.

But in September you get a letter from your sister. "Our hopes for a good potato crop are gone. The potatoes are no larger than marbles."

Your heart aches. If your family starves, it will be your fault. You should have been saving money and sending it home instead of spending it all. From now on, you vow to save every penny. You still see your pals in the Black Crows from time to time, but your partying days are over for now.

Over the next two years, you send tickets to Ireland. One by one, your brothers join you. Together, you'll bring the rest of the family to New York. It took a letter to remind you of your promise, but now nothing can stop you.

THE END

To follow another path, turn to page 11.
To read the conclusion, turn to page 101.

Curious onlookers gathered to
watch firefighters battle flames.

Even with your shirt around her shoulders,
the young woman shivers in the cold night air.
"How can I help?" you ask.

She thrusts the baby into your arms. "I'll be
back," she says as she dashes away.

The fire eventually dies out. The crowd
goes home, leaving you standing alone in the
middle of the street holding a damp baby.

The baby coughs. You touch his cheek. He's burning up. He coughs again, opens his eyes, and is about to howl when you feel his mother tug at your elbow. "I'll take him," she says. "My friend says we can stay the night with her." She tries to return your shirt, but you tell her to keep it. She needs it more than you do.

Turn the page.

It's very late when you return to the apartment and fall into bed. As the week goes on, you begin to feel sick. Your head aches. Kate puts a hand to your head. "You're burning up." She places a cold cloth on your head. "We should take you to the hospital."

"It's probably a cold." You remember the baby coughing on the night of the fire. If you spend money on a hospital visit, you'll have less to send home to your family. "I'll be fine," you say.

You stay in bed for another week with a fever, chills, and a hacking cough. One morning you look into Kate's eyes and think she's your mother. Are you in Ireland?

No. You are a victim of a typhus epidemic. Many recover, but you are not among them. Your family won't be able to rely on you to help them survive the famine. They'll have to start over to make their dream of getting to America a reality.

THE END

To follow another path, turn to page 11.
To read the conclusion, turn to page 101.

Crowds of people waited by the docks to reunite with their family members and friends.

You're more determined than ever to get the rest of your family to America. After months of saving, you send two tickets to Ireland. In the next letter from home, you learn that your brother and your sister will arrive in May, one year after you reached America. You save enough to rent an apartment to share with them.

When she sees you, your sister covers your face with kisses. Your brother gives you a bear hug. "It was a rough trip. Several passengers died," he says.

Your brother finds work at a construction site carting bricks. It's a start. "Someday," he says, "I'll own the brickyard."

Turn the page.

Immigrant families squeezed
into small tenement apartments.

For money, your sister washes other people's
dirty clothes. Her fingers turn red from
scrubbing. "Someday I'll own my own house,
and then I'll hire someone to do my laundry."

In America, you can dream big. Your biggest
dream is bringing the rest of the family to join
you there.

THE END

To follow another path, turn to page 11.
To read the conclusion, turn to page 101.

The shopkeeper plans to leave for California in one week. "Don't worry about a thing. I'll pay for your boat ticket. When we set up a store in California, we'll be rich beyond our wildest dreams."

You send $20 to your family in Ireland. They need it more than you do. Maybe Father will send one of your brothers to America. Then two of you will be earning good wages.

You help the shopkeeper load shirts, blankets, boots, and rolls of cloth into a wagon for the trip to the pier. You'll be sailing around the southern tip of South America. What a great adventure!

THE END

To follow another path, turn to page 11.
To read the conclusion, turn to page 101.

These young women worked in Lowell's cotton mills in the 1800s.

LIFE IN LOWELL

Mary and Eliza Kelly are happy when you tell them you'll be joining them in Lowell, Massachusetts. You spend your last $5 buying your ticket to Lowell.

When you arrive, the three of you hurry to one of the mill's boarding houses. Six girls share each bedroom, two to a bed. The Kelly sisters sleep together. You share a bed with Becky, a farm girl from Vermont.

Faint morning light shines through the window as Becky shakes you awake. "Work begins at 5:00 sharp," she says.

You follow Becky to the second floor of one of the mills. The windows are nailed shut, and the room is hot. Lint flies in your face and gets into your nose and throat. Machines screech and make the floor shake.

As a spinner, Becky spins cotton strands into thread. Spools turn the thread onto bobbins. Your job is to take the full bobbins off the machines and replace them with empty bobbins.

You drop a bobbin. Becky gives you an encouraging smile, but the supervisor shouts a warning. "The metal teeth on those machines will crush your fingers and yank out your hair if you're not careful," he says.

The workday ends at 7:00 that evening. Your head throbs, your ears ring, and your legs ache. You collapse into bed.

Large power looms like this
one had many gears with
dangerous metal teeth.

Turn the page.

On payday Becky receives $2.33 after the cost of room and board. You've only worked part of a week, so you earn less.

Everyone heads to town. Becky is going to the bookshop. The Kelly sisters want to buy combs and hairpins. Will you go with Becky or with Mary and Eliza?

➳ To go with Becky to the bookshop, go to page **49**.

➳ To go with Mary and Eliza to the general store, turn to page **51**.

You and Becky browse through books in B.C. Sargent's Bookshop. The store smells of fine paper and new books. But you don't buy any for yourself. You want to save every cent you can. The more you save, the sooner you can send tickets home to your family.

As you and Becky leave the store, you see a notice about an upcoming speech. On Thursday night, a woman will be speaking about colleges for women.

"Just think," Becky says. "Perhaps we could become teachers." The two of you make plans to attend the lecture.

At the mill the next day, someone hands you a leaflet about a labor union meeting scheduled for Thursday night. "What's a union?" you ask Becky.

Turn the page.

"A labor union is a group of workers who try to improve work conditions," she says. "The union wants 10-hour workdays and better wages."

"I would like that," you reply.

"The union wants to have a strike. But the last time they tried that, the owners didn't give in. The girls had to go back to work for less money, not more."

"But there must be some way to improve conditions at the mill," you say.

"Go to the union meeting if you'd like," Becky says. "I'd rather learn about women's colleges."

Which will you attend?

➤ *To go to the lecture, turn to page 54.*

➤ *To go to the union meeting, turn to page 61.*

Shops and businesses lined the streets of Lowell.

Mary and Eliza lead you to Louis Tower's shop. As you enter, the smells of soaps, lotions, and perfumes hang in the air. You want to smell good, too. There are not enough bathhouses in Lowell, so you choose some perfume to make you smell sweet. Mary and Eliza buy combs and hairpins.

Turn the page.

Back at the boarding house, you read Becky's copy of the *Lowell Advertiser*. An ad for a maid catches your interest. Maybe you should apply. You hate the loud clanging of the mill machines.

Workers gathered in front of Boott Cotton Mills in Lowell.

When you tell Becky what you have in mind, she warns you. "Mill girls have much more free time than maids. In the evenings, we attend classes, read, shop, or visit. Maids don't have time for any of that."

"Classes?" you ask.

"Some of the mill girls have saved enough to go to college," Becky says. "I'm going to a lecture Thursday about women's colleges. Why don't you join me?"

"I've always dreamed of being a teacher," you say.

But you're tired. Mill work is exhausting. It might be nicer to work in a clean, quiet house on a tree-lined street.

➤ To go to the lecture, turn to page 54.

➤ To apply for the maid's job, turn to page 58.

The lecture room is full of girls from the mill. Everyone has a book with her, and when the speaker enters, they put the books aside and begin taking notes.

The speaker says that she used to be a mill girl. Now, thanks to the Troy Female Seminary in Troy, New York, she's a teacher. You wonder if you could become a teacher, too.

You decide to become a teacher, but you don't forget your family. For every dollar you save for college, you put another aside to send to Ireland. You spend very little on yourself. You buy a notebook and pen, but you don't buy books. You borrow them from the library on Merrimack Street.

Many businesses could be found on Merrimack Street, shown here in 1896.

Turn the page.

While you save for college, you also send money to Ireland. One by one, your brothers and sisters come to America.

By working hard at the mill, you earn a better job as a spinner, then as a weaver. One day your supervisor takes you aside. "I have an opening for a floor supervisor. Are you interested?"

Weavers wove threads together on looms to make fabric.

That night you can't sleep. As a supervisor, perhaps you can improve the conditions in the mill. You'll treat workers kindly and convince the owners to shorten work hours.

But you have finally saved enough to pay for college. As a teacher, you'll help other immigrants get good educations. With better education, they could get better jobs.

Should you follow your dream and go to school? Or should you stay at the mill and help the other workers?

→ To go to college, turn to page **74**.
→ To become a supervisor, turn to page **77**.

The newspaper ad leads you to a large house with green shutters and lace curtains. You knock on the door nervously. A woman answers the door.

"I need someone to do laundry and help Cook," she says. "You'll earn $2 a week and share a room with Cook."

Cook is tough, but fair. If you don't do the job right, Cook makes you do it over. You smile when she sings Irish songs off-key as she stirs the soup.

You dust and polish the furniture weekly and keep the wooden floor as clean as the dining room table. When you have a home of your own, you'll keep it as neat and clean as this one.

Lowell's wealthy residents lived in large houses in the city.

Turn the page.

Cook's son, Thomas, walks his mother to church every Sunday. Going to church every Sunday with Cook and Thomas becomes the highlight of your week.

One day, you and Tom go on a picnic. As you sit by the river, Tom asks you to marry him. "I have a good job. Once we're married, you can quit yours."

Turn to page 64.

At the union meeting, one woman tells you that the group plans to send a message to the Massachusetts government requesting a 10-hour workday. "Will you sign?" she asks.

But before you can answer, a speaker at the front of the room declares, "Now that the Irish are coming over, our wages will be even lower. They're desperate for work. They'll accept any pay."

You don't say anything, but the comment makes you uneasy. Are they saying the low pay is your fault? You leave without signing, determined to prove that Irish immigrants are good workers.

Turn the page.

Almost all mill workers
were women or girls.

Life takes on a regular rhythm. Soon you
join Becky as a spinner. You never get used to
the stink of the oil lamps that light the mill in
winter. The cotton lint falls in the workroom
like snow.

You develop a cough. Becky urges you to go to a doctor. "It could be serious."

But it might just be a cold. You have almost enough money to send a ticket to Ireland. If you spend it on doctors and medicine, you'll have nothing left.

→ To save your money, turn to page **68**.

→ To go to the doctor, turn to page **72**.

When you were a young girl in Ireland, you dreamed of marrying a man like Tom and having a house full of children and laughter. But once the potato crops failed, such a happy future was hard to believe.

Are you ready to give up your job? You enjoy earning money of your own. Besides, if you marry Tom and quit your job, where will you get the money to bring your family to America?

➻ To accept Tom's proposal, turn to page **76**.

➻ To turn down Tom's proposal, go to page **65**.

Saying no to Tom is one of the most difficult things you have ever done. But a letter from your sister in Ireland tells you that you made the right decision. She writes, "Everyone misses you. There is little to eat, so we survive on cabbages. Cabbages fill the empty places, but make our stomachs ache."

You feel uncomfortable around Cook after saying no to Tom, so you take a different housekeeping job nearby.

Turn the page.

The next month, you send your sister a ticket along with a letter. "I am living with a very nice family," you write. "My mistress is so concerned about my health that she makes me wear boots to go outside in the wet grass. You'll have a job here, too. Come soon."

Irish women often took jobs as maids or cooks.

When your sister finally arrives, you hug, cry, and dance a jig. Together, you send more tickets to Ireland. Each family member who arrives finds a job to pay for the next person to make the trip from Ireland to America. Before too long, your family is together again.

THE END

To follow another path, turn to page 11.
To read the conclusion, turn to page 101.

You can live with a cough. Your family in Ireland is starving. They need your earnings more than you need a doctor.

Every time you enter the mill, you begin to wheeze and cough. You feel short of breath. Some days you struggle to climb the stairs to work.

It's a proud day in February when you send two tickets to Ireland. Your brother and sister arrive in May, one year after you. They sail directly to Boston and take the train from there to Lowell. They are tired and dirty, but healthy. They tell you that many other travelers on the crowded ship had become very ill.

"You look wonderful to me," you say, giving them both big hugs.

Poor conditions on crowded ships made many people ill by the time they arrived in America.

Turn the page.

"Are you all right?" they ask. "You look very pale."

You try to hide your cough. "Don't worry. I'll be fine."

As time goes on, your breathing becomes more and more difficult. You finally go to the doctor who treats mill workers.

"It's called brown lung disease," he says. "The cotton fibers irritate your lungs. There's no treatment. All you can do is stop working in the mills. You may or may not recover fully. But you'll feel better."

You decide not to tell your brother and sister. With three of you working, you'll soon be able to bring the rest of the family to America. If you quit, it will just take longer. So you keep on working, despite your wheezing and hacking cough.

Over time, the three of you make enough money to buy tickets for the whole family. The thought of everyone being together again brings you great joy. But you won't be there to greet them. You die of lung disease a few weeks before they arrive.

On their first night in America, your family cooks a large supper. They finally have food to fill their stomachs. But your death has left an empty place at the dinner table and in their hearts.

THE END

To follow another path, turn to page 11.
To read the conclusion, turn to page 101.

The doctor says you have brown lung disease. "It comes from breathing lint in the mills. You'll have to quit working there. If you stay, your cough will get worse, and then you'll begin to wheeze. Eventually, this disease will kill you."

"Where will I go?" you ask, but the doctor has no answer.

You return to the boarding house to tell the keeper that you have to leave. She reports that Mrs. Sargent, whose husband owns the bookshop, needs a girl to help with laundry and cooking.

Mrs. Sargent hires you immediately. Your cough clears up, and you find that you enjoy working for the Sargents. When you write home, you enclose a few dollars. Next time you write, perhaps you'll be able to send a ticket, maybe even two. What a grand day that will be!

THE END

To follow another path, turn to page 11.
To read the conclusion, turn to page 101.

You're too close to your dream of becoming a teacher to give up now. A few months later, you leave Lowell and go to Mount Holyoke Female Seminary in South Hadley, Massachusetts. Tuition is $60 a year.

Mount Holyoke was founded in 1837 and is still open today.

While you are in school, your brothers and sisters work to send money back to Ireland. By the time you graduate, your whole family is there to celebrate with you. You are the first college graduate—and the first teacher—in your family. Someday there will be others.

THE END

To follow another path, turn to page 11.
To read the conclusion, turn to page 101.

As soon as you say yes to Tom, you go tell Cook. She hugs you. "I know you'll be happy," she cries.

You write home with the good news and dream of the day when you'll have your own home with lace curtains at the windows. Somehow you'll find a way to send money to Ireland. It will simply take longer than you had hoped.

THE END

To follow another path, turn to page 11.
To read the conclusion, turn to page 101.

As a supervisor, you try to make life better for the workers on your floor, but you find you can't change the long hours or low pay.

With the money you had saved for college, you send tickets to the rest of your family. Together, you all rent a big apartment in the Acre, an Irish section of Lowell.

What a happy day it is when your family is all together again. You hug, kiss, eat, drink, sing, and hear stories of the journey. Your oldest brothers and sisters find jobs. The little ones go to school. You all work hard to have a good life in America.

THE END

To follow another path, turn to page 11.
To read the conclusion, turn to page 101.

Crowded storefronts lined
the streets of Philadelphia
in the mid-1800s.

CHAPTER 4

INDUSTRY IN PENNSYLVANIA

Will, Mary, and Eliza wish you well. Then you all head off in different directions. You see the lights of Philadelphia long before the train pulls into the station.

"Welcome," Brian says when you arrive. He lives in a three-story brick house, connected to the houses on either side. It's very narrow and quite small. There's one room on each floor.

Brian introduces you to his wife, Ellen, who shows you through the house and to your attic room. "I hope you'll be comfortable," Ellen says.

Turn the page.

Brian tells you that row houses like his cost about $300. "Lots of Irish in Philadelphia own homes. Someday you will too."

You hope so, but first you have to find a job. "The railroad is looking for workers," Brian says. "There are thousands of miles of tracks to lay."

Brian's neighbor says that Morris Iron Works on 7th Street is hiring, too. You don't know enough about these jobs to choose wisely, but you must choose.

➤ *To work for the railroad, go to page* **81**.

➤ *To work at Morris Iron Works, turn to page* **84**.

You join dozens of men standing in line at the railroad office. All are eager for work. The man next to you says the railroad needs men to dig paths for new tracks. "They pay less than a dollar a day. But it's work."

At the tracks, the boss gives you a shovel. You dig until you think you cannot dig anymore. One man faints from the heat. Another stumbles and twists his ankle. He keeps on digging anyway.

Turn the page.

Payday comes once a month. You've worked six days each week for more than 12 hours a day. When you reach the head of the line, you are given almost $3 less than you expected. But when you stop to question the boss, your friend pushes you along.

Expanding railroads provided jobs for immigrants.

"Complaining is a bad idea. They say one wage, but they pay another. We can't do anything about it, not if we want to keep our jobs," he says. "That's why I go to the pub on payday. Being with friends helps me forget my troubles. Why don't you come with me?"

"I'd like to go, but I promised my cousin I'd be home for supper. They've planned something special."

→ *To go to the pub with your friend, turn to page 87.*

→ *To go back to Brian's, turn to page 89.*

Philadelphia is a manufacturing city. Huge factories belch soot. The pounding of big machines hammers the air. When you open the door at the Morris Iron Works, a blast of heat nearly sends you back outside. Smoke burns your eyes.

Men on overhead runways dump charcoal and iron ore into a giant furnace. Red-hot metal pours out from a door at the bottom of the furnace. The metal is pig iron. Blacksmiths will turn it into rails for the trains.

The boss asks if you are a blacksmith. You shake your head no. He waves you out the door, but another man pulls you aside.

"I need someone to carry ingots," he says. "I'll pay 80 cents a day, and I expect you to work six days a week."

Piles of steel ingots filled the stockyard at this steel company in Coatesville, Pennsylvania.

The man explains that ingots are bars of cooled metal. "Each ingot weighs about 50 pounds. A cartful is heavy, but we have to move them out of the factory to the railroad car. I hope you have a strong back."

Turn the page.

After 14 hours, you are exhausted, but you return the next day ready to haul more ingots. The first weeks are hard, but you get used to the work.

Each payday, you give Brian money toward your food and room. You put the rest aside to send to Ireland.

One night, your friend is headed to the pub. "Come along. We'll have fun." But Brian and Ellen are expecting you. Will they understand if you don't come right home?

➤ *To go with your friend to the pub,*
go to page **87**.

➤ *To return to Brian's, turn to page* **89**.

The pub is full of Irish immigrants. As you buy a drink and some food, everyone welcomes you to America.

They tell you about a group called The Society of the Sons of St. Patrick trying to help the Irish. "They send food and money to Ireland."

"If this year's potato crop fails, people are sure to starve," one man says.

Everyone complains about their wages. "We're no better off than slaves," they say. Several of the men are heading to Scranton to work in the coal mines. "The pay is good. I say we should give it a try."

Turn the page.

Maybe you'd earn more in Scranton than in Philadelphia. Maybe mining will be easier than what you are doing now. With the higher wages, you'll be able to send money home faster.

On the other hand, you like Philadelphia and enjoy staying with Brian and Ellen. Will you go to Scranton or stay where you are?

➤ *To go to Scranton, turn to page* **91**.

➤ *To stay in Philadelphia, turn to page* **95**.

Brian's house is packed with neighbors who have come to meet you. Ellen's stew is a hit. One man plays a fiddle, and the party spills into the street for dancing. You feel at home among these friendly Irish neighbors.

The next Sunday, Brian and Ellen invite you to join them for services at Holy Trinity Church. After the service, people share news from Ireland, tell stories, and gossip.

Brian introduces you to John Murphy. Murphy came from Ireland in 1833 as a blacksmith. Now he and his business partner, William C. Allison, build railroad cars and streetcars. "Come work for me at the Allison Manufacturing Company," he says. "I can't promise high wages, but I'll treat you right."

Turn the page.

It's tempting. You like Murphy. Maybe you should change jobs.

On the other hand, you won't be paid for the last week's work. You'll have worked 84 hours for nothing! Is Murphy's offer worth losing a week's income?

➤ *To work for Murphy,
turn to page* **93**.

➤ *To stay at your current job,
turn to page* **95**.

Housing provided by mining companies was often run-down.

When you report to the mining company, the boss gives you a place to live. "The rent comes out of your wages. You can buy what you need at the company store," he says.

The boss explains that skilled miners dig the coal. Your job is to pick it up off the ground deep inside the earth. Once your cart is full, you push it out of the mine. Then you go back and get more.

Turn the page.

On payday, you line up to get your wages. You expect to get $24, but you only get $12. The company took the rest for rent and supplies you bought at the company store.

You stop to talk to a friend about your small paycheck. Another miner comes running up. "Did you hear? There's been another accident. A man fell under a cart full of coal. He's dead."

Your friend shakes his head. "Accidents happen too often. I'm leaving. I don't plan to die in the mines. California is the place to go. It's a land of sunshine and opportunity. Join me if you want."

→ *To stay in the mines, turn to page* **97**.

→ *To go to California, turn to page* **99**.

On Monday morning, you report to John Murphy at the Allison Manufacturing Company. Murphy puts you to work tending the fires at his blacksmith forge. The work is hot and hard, but Murphy treats you well.

Blacksmiths melted iron at forges before converting it into steel.

Turn the page.

You show up every day ready to work hard. After a few months, Murphy gives you a raise and assigns you more important jobs.

In November, you have enough for two tickets to America from Ireland. You borrow money from the local building and loan association to buy a house. It will take years to repay them, but now you have a place for your family to live when they arrive.

Your brother and sister arrive in June. You help them find work. "We're all working now," your brother says. "If we put our earnings together, we'll bring the others here in no time."

THE END

To follow another path, turn to page 11.
To read the conclusion, turn to page 101.

You return to your job, but you're not sure you made the right decision. Your back aches, and you are tired all the time.

When your sister writes that they are facing sure starvation, you send her a few more dollars. You don't write that you are sick of breaking your back for 14 hours a day or that your bosses treat you worse than a dog. At least you have enough to eat.

Turn the page.

After five months, you have saved enough to send a ticket to Ireland.

Your sister arrives in July 1847. She finds a job as a maid in a big house on Walnut Street. "Someday," she says, "we'll own a house of our own. But first we'll bring Mother, Father, and the rest to America."

THE END

To follow another path, turn to page 11.
To read the conclusion, turn to page 101.

You decide to continue working in the mine. As soon as you've saved $20, you send it to Brian. He'll buy a ticket and send it to your family in Ireland. If you use the mining company bank, they'll take a share as payment for the service.

You work, you eat, you sleep. You have neither time nor energy for anything else.

As you walk to work one morning in October, you admire the colorful fall leaves. You enjoy the rays of summer sun on your face. Then you go down into the mine.

You are picking up a load of coal from deep inside the mine when you hear someone yell, "Get out!"

Turn the page.

Horses helped pull cartloads of coal from inside the mine.

But it's too late. The mine collapses, and you are buried beneath a flood of coal. The sun may be shining outside, but you die in darkness. Your dream of getting the rest of the family to America is crushed.

THE END

To follow another path, turn to page 11.
To read the conclusion, turn to page 101.

You write a letter to Ireland telling the family that you are heading west. You promise to send word and money as soon as you are settled.

It will be a long journey to California. But you've already come a long way. You are as excited as when you boarded the ship from Ireland one year ago. You have $12 in your pocket. It won't get you far, but you'll find work along the way. Full of hope, you set out in search of a new life.

THE END

To follow another path, turn to page 11.
To read the conclusion, turn to page 101.

For many Irish people, sailing to America was the only way to escape starvation.

CHAPTER 5

IRISH AMERICANS

The Irish brought their dreams to America to escape a nightmare back home. Beginning in 1845, a terrible blight struck Ireland's potato crops. Without warning, about one-third of the potatoes rotted. Many Irish, who were used to eating 6 to 14 pounds of potatoes each day, suddenly had no food.

The problem only got worse. In 1846, nearly half of the crop was lost. In 1847, the entire crop rotted. By the time the famine ended, about 1.5 million Irish people had died.

Those who could raise the money bought tickets to America. Between 1845 and 1855, about 1.8 million Irish people left Ireland for North America. Most had little choice. If they stayed in Ireland, they would starve.

Irish immigrants in America sent money and tickets to their relatives in Ireland. In 1846, immigrants sent about $1 million to Ireland. By 1850, they had sent nearly $5 million, even though many were working in low-paying jobs.

Irish immigrants tended to create Irish neighborhoods within American cities. Newcomers felt most comfortable with other Irish people. New York, Boston, Philadelphia, Chicago, and New Orleans were favorite places for Irish immigrants to settle.

Most Irish immigrants arrived in America without money. They took any jobs they could find, often working long hours for low wages. Men dug canals, built railroads, and worked in mines. Irish women often worked as servants. Others worked in factories, like cotton mills. Dangerous work, poor nutrition, and crowded housing led many to an early death.

Irish immigrants in America set up aid societies to help newcomers.

Religion and faith provided support for struggling immigrants. Irish immigrants attended Catholic churches. They also set up Catholic schools and aid societies to help new arrivals.

Despite the struggles, many Irish immigrants prospered and made a good life in America. Irish immigrants bought houses, set up businesses, and sent their children to school. They became leaders in business, education, and politics. The United States gave the Irish immigrants opportunities that they would not have had in Ireland.

Irish immigrants changed America. They brought new ideas, a strong faith, and the determination to make the United States a better place for everyone.

TIME LINE

1845—Irish farmers discover the first signs of the potato blight. More than one-third of the potato crop rots.

1845–1855—About 1.8 million Irish come to the United States.

1846—More than half of the Irish potato crop rots.

1846–1850—As many as 1.5 million people die in Ireland during the famine.

1847—Nearly all of the potato crop is lost.

1848—About one-third of the Irish potato crop is lost.

1849—Thousands of Irish immigrants go to California for the gold rush.

1850—Eighty percent of the 1.6 million Catholics in the U.S. are foreign-born.

1850–1860—The number of Catholic churches in Philadelphia doubles.

1852—Half of the mill workers in Lowell, Massachusetts, are Irish.

1853—Irish workers building the Erie Railroad strike for higher wages. They want $1.25 for a 10-hour day.

1861–1865—About 150,000 Irish immigrants fight for the Union in the Civil War.

1870s—Irish-Americans gain political power in New York, Boston, Chicago, and other major cities.

OTHER PATHS TO EXPLORE

In this book, you've seen how the experiences of Irish immigrants were different from three points of view.

Perspectives on history are as varied as the people who lived it. You can explore other paths on your own to learn more about what happened. Seeing history from many points of view is an important part of understanding it.

Here are some ideas for other Irish immigration points of view to explore:

+ Irish immigrants often left their families behind when they traveled to America. What was it like to stay in Ireland during the famine?

+ At first, Irish immigrants had little political power. But by sticking together as a group, they slowly gained power in city politics. What was it like for an immigrant to become the first Irish mayor of a large city?

+ Cotton mills, mining companies, and other businesses paid very low wages to Irish workers. If you were a business owner in the late 1800s, how would you treat immigrant workers?

READ MORE

Bartoletti, Susan Campbell. *Black Potatoes: The Story of the Great Irish Famine, 1845–1850.* Boston: Houghton Mifflin, 2001.

O'Hara, Megan. *Irish Immigrants 1840–1920.* Mankato, Minn.: Blue Earth Books, 2002.

Paulson, Timothy J. *Irish Immigrants.* New York: Facts on File, 2005.

Thornton, Jeremy. *The Irish Potato Famine: Irish Immigrants Come to America (1845–1850).* New York: PowerKids Press, 2004.

INTERNET SITES

FactHound offers a safe, fun way to find Internet sites related to this book. All of the sites on FactHound have been researched by our staff.

Here's how:

1. Visit *www.facthound.com*
2. Choose your grade level.
3. Type in this book ID **1429601612** for age-appropriate sites. You may also browse subjects by clicking on letters, or by clicking on pictures and words.
4. Click on the **Fetch It** button.

FactHound will fetch the best sites for you!

GLOSSARY

blight (BLITE)—a disease that destroys plants

bobbin (BOB-in)—a spool inside a sewing machine or on a loom that holds the thread

epidemic (ep-uh-DEM-ik)—an infectious disease that spreads quickly through a population

famine (FAM-uhn)—a serious shortage of food resulting in widespread hunger and death

immigrant (IM-uh-gruhnt)—someone who comes from abroad to live permanently in a new country

pub (PUHB)—a place where people come to socialize, eat, and drink

tenement (TEN-uh-muhnt)—a run-down apartment building, especially one that is crowded and in a poor part of a city

typhus (TYE-fuhss)—a severe disease that causes fever, headache, weakness, coughing, and a dark red rash

union (YOON-yuhn)—an organized group of workers that tries to gain better pay and working conditions for workers

BIBLIOGRAPHY

Anbinder, Tyler. *Five Points: The 19th-Century New York City Neighborhood That Invented Tap Dance, Stole Elections, and Became the World's Most Notorious Slum.* New York: The Free Press, 2001.

Clark, Dennis. *The Irish in Philadelphia: Ten Generations of Urban Experience.* Philadelphia: Temple University Press, 1973.

Laxton, Edward. *The Famine Ships: The Irish Exodus to America.* New York: Henry Holt, 1997.

Miller, Kerby A. *Emigrants and Exiles: Ireland and the Irish Exodus to North America.* New York: Oxford University Press, 1985.

Moran, William. *The Belles of New England: The Women of the Textile Mills and the Families Whose Wealth They Wove.* New York: Thomas Dunne Books/St. Martin's Press, 2002.

Potter, George W. *To the Golden Door: The Story of the Irish in Ireland and America.* Boston: Little, Brown, 1960.

Robinson, Harriet H. *Loom and Spindle or Life Among the Early Mill Girls.* Kailua, Hawaii: Press Pacifica, 1976.

INDEX